Carrie,

EAT
DRINK
&
BE
SNARKY

a sweary adult coloring book for brides

shannon campbell

Eat, Drink, and Be Snarky: A Sweary Adult Coloring Book for Brides

Please let it be
noted that this book
was gifted to Connie Yee
to help preserve her
mental health while
planning her glorious
wedding to Bobo!

F' the Small Stuff
ENJOY the MOMENTS!

Fuck *that* shit.

That's something I found myself saying a lot when I was planning my wedding last year. I couldn't make a move without being clobbered by someone's strong, unsolicited opinion about the **dumbest** shit, like the absorbency of the cocktail napkins, where my terrible cousins were going to sit, how much wine I should be allowed to drink, ad NAUSEUM. I mean, barf. I sort of felt like screaming:

everybody,

get

off

my

shit.

But I couldn't. Because, you know, **they all mean well**. And they probably love the hell out of you. That's the tough shit with a wedding. It's the best day of your life with all your favorite people, but sometimes it will also kill you a little inside.

So every time you quite earnestly do not give a fuck about the current decision (and also when you give a huge fuck but no one is getting it), pick up this coloring book and vent out some of that screaminess. Because there's a bridezilla in every single one of us, and honestly, you are a real boss bitch for even holding it together this far.

And remember--honeymoon's almost here! You're gonna make it.

Cheers to your (and no one else's!) special day,
Shannon

P.S. If this makes your planning a little less painful, leave me a review on Amazon! It will help the next bride find this book and color herself back to sanity.

Time to test those colors! (Because no one can do it right but you anyway.)

color test grid

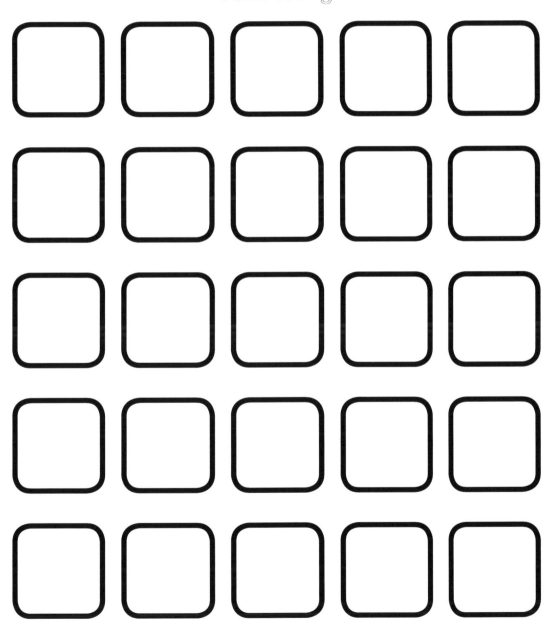

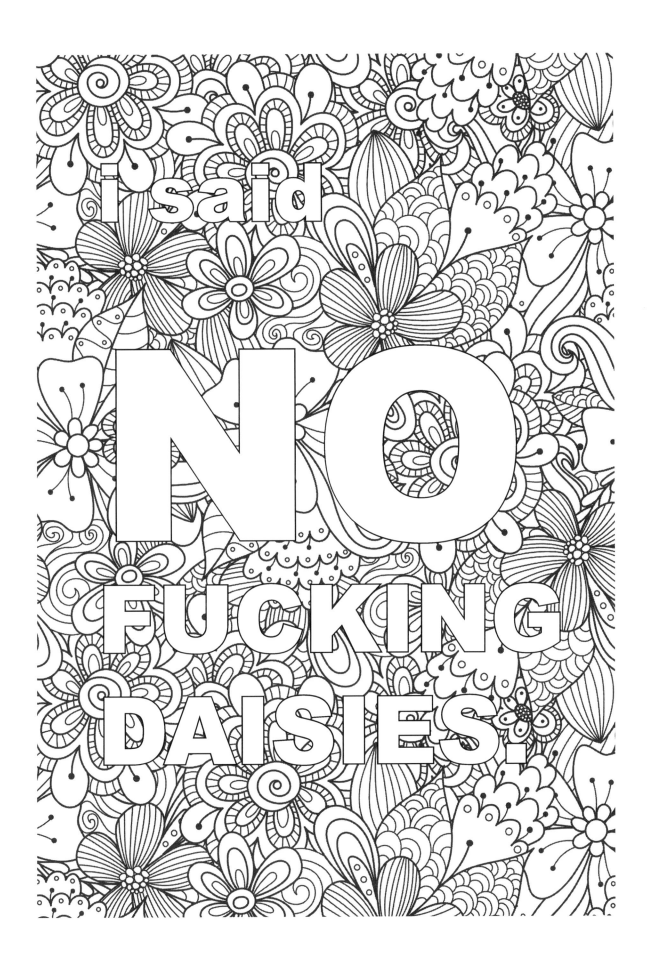

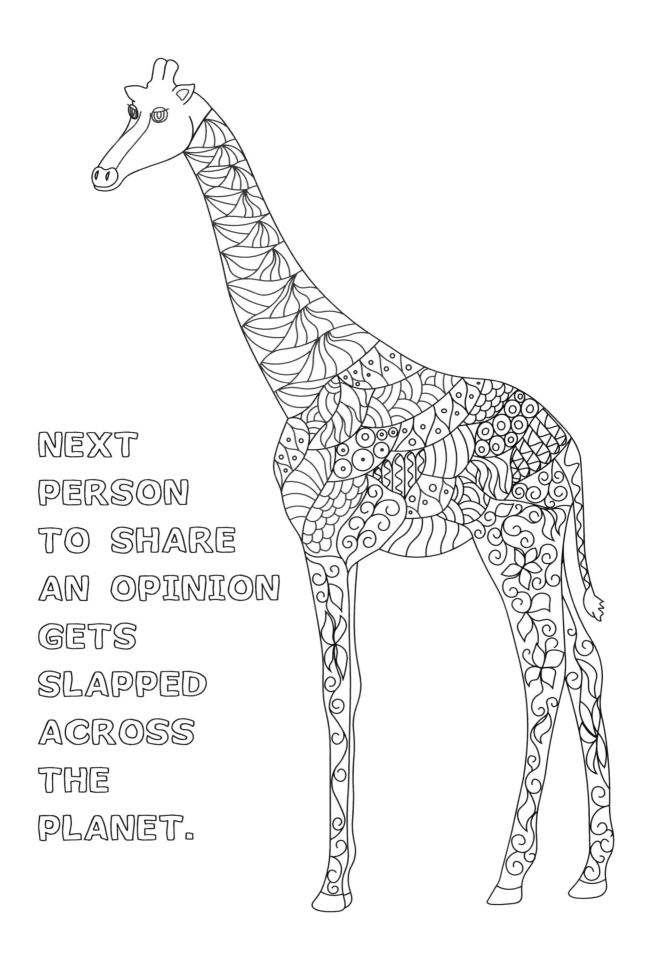

NEXT
PERSON
TO SHARE
AN OPINION
GETS
SLAPPED
ACROSS
THE
PLANET.

Actually,

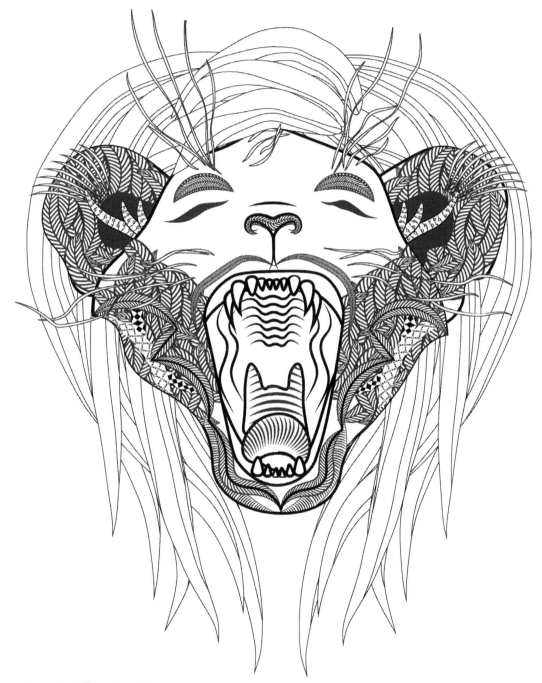

YOU are a bridezilla,
BITCH.

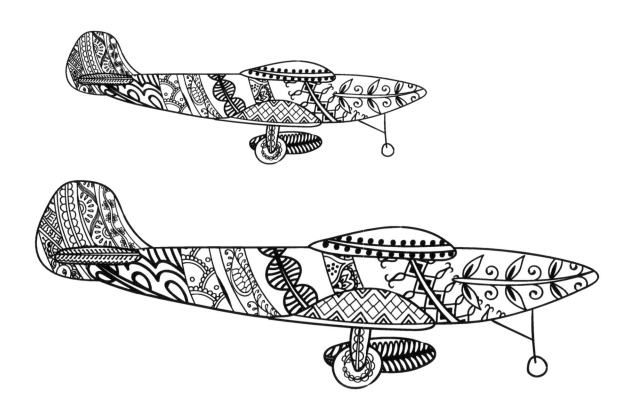

Time to
send Uncle Ed
a thank you
bomb.

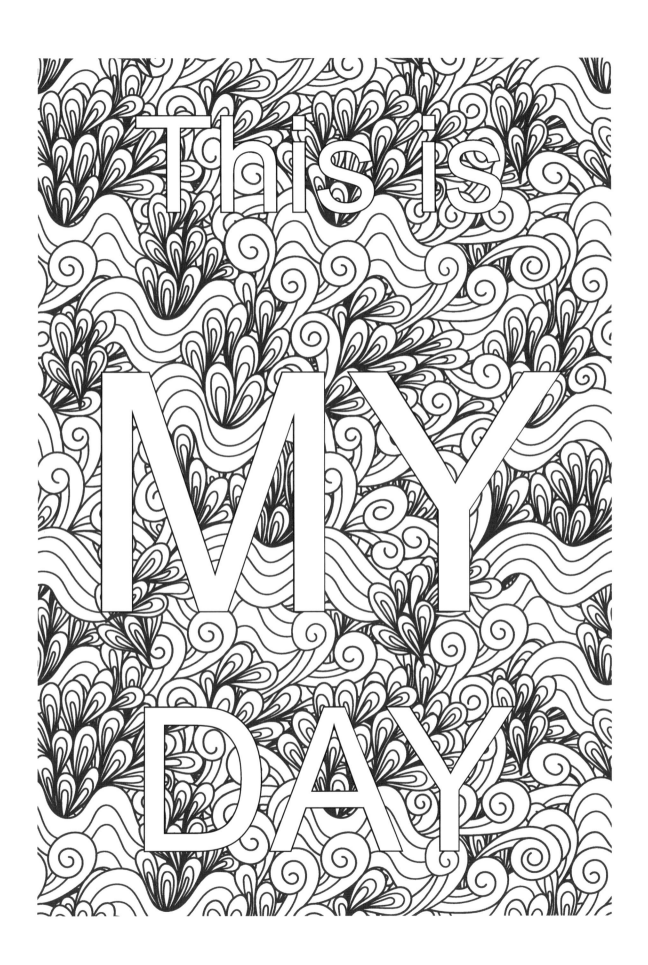

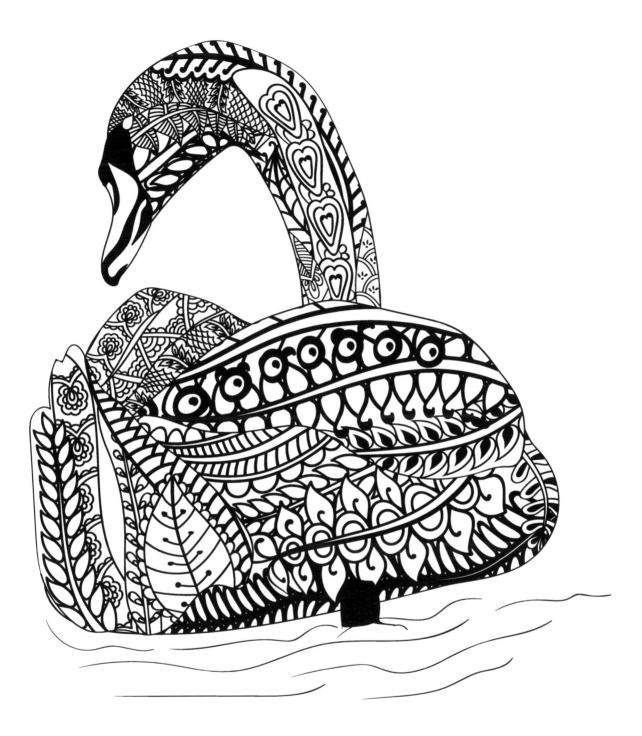

I will stab the next person
who speaks to me.

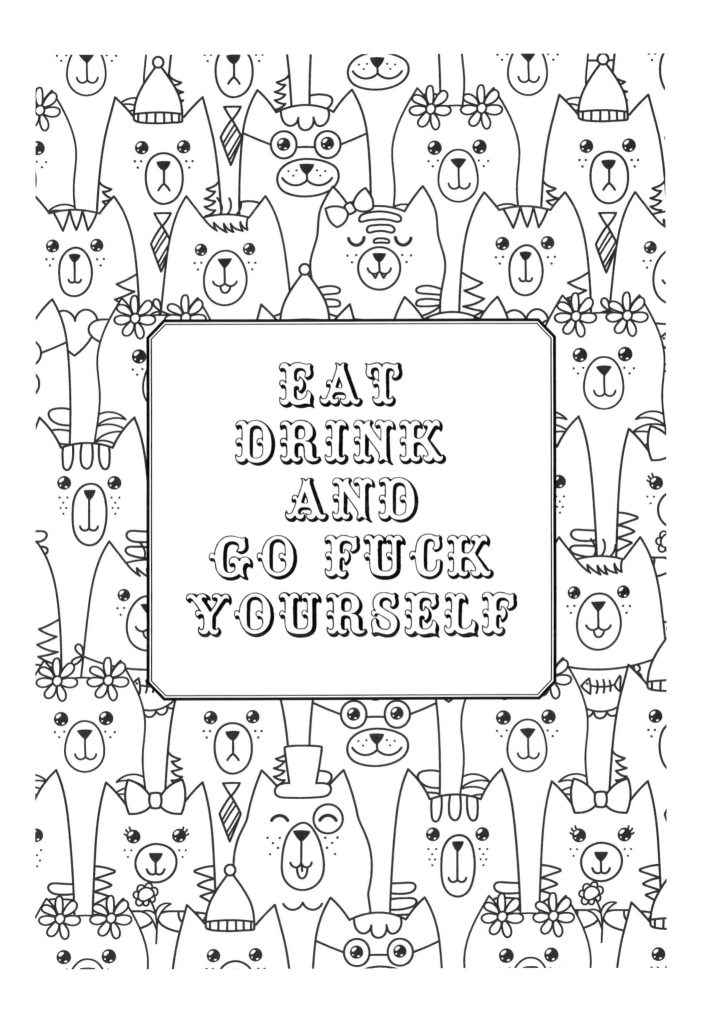

THE CIRCLE OF NO.

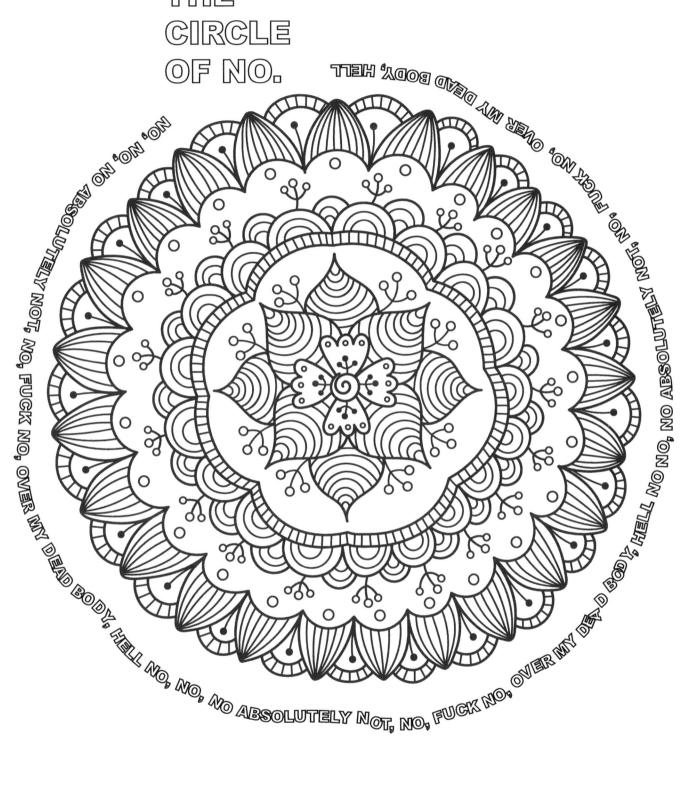

NO, NO, ABSOLUTELY NOT, NO, FUCK NO, OVER MY DEAD BODY, HELL NO, NO, NO ABSOLUTELY NOT, NO, FUCK NO, OVER MY DEAD BODY, HELL NO, NO, NO ABSOLUTELY NOT, NO, FUCK NO, OVER MY DEAD BODY, HELL NO, NO, NO ABSOLUTELY NOT, NO, FUCK NO, OVER MY DEAD BODY, HELL

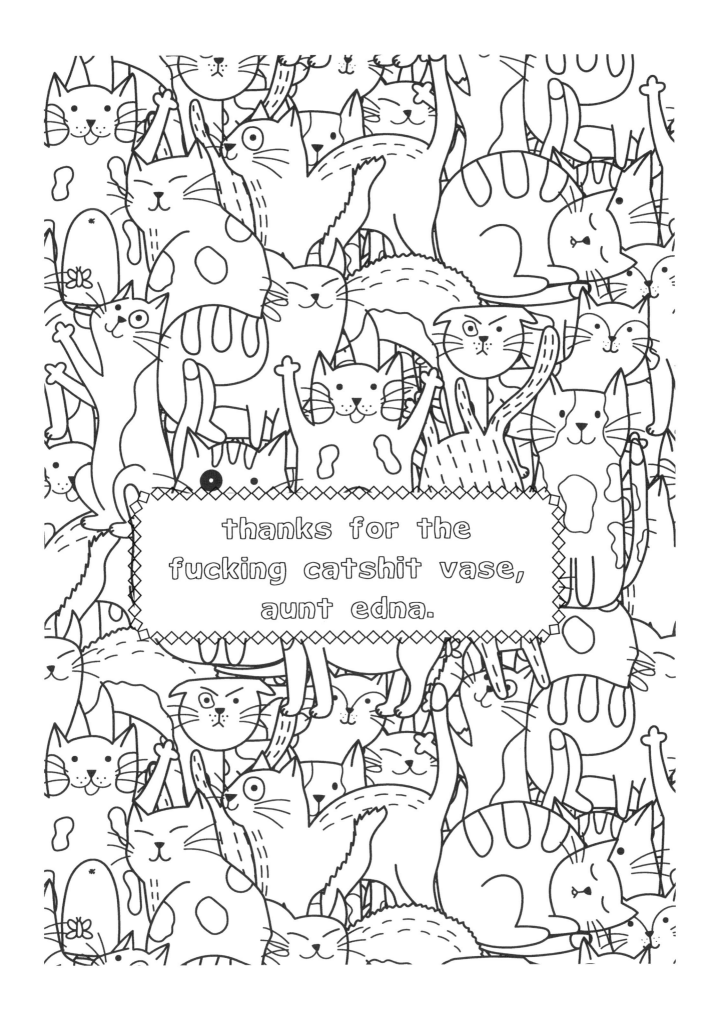

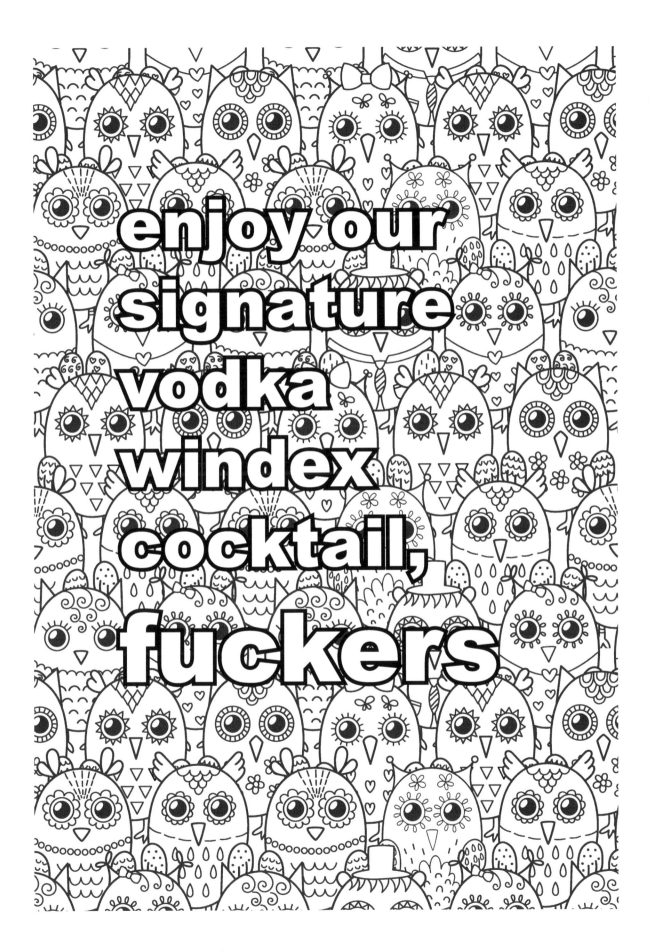

enjoy our
signature
vodka
windex
cocktail,
fuckers

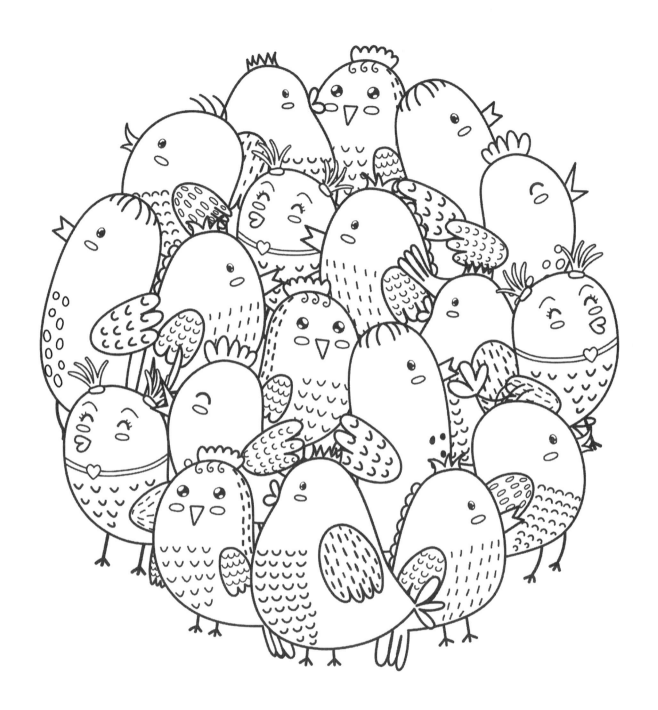

Your shitfactory
children are cordially
not invited.

Zen as a motherfucker.

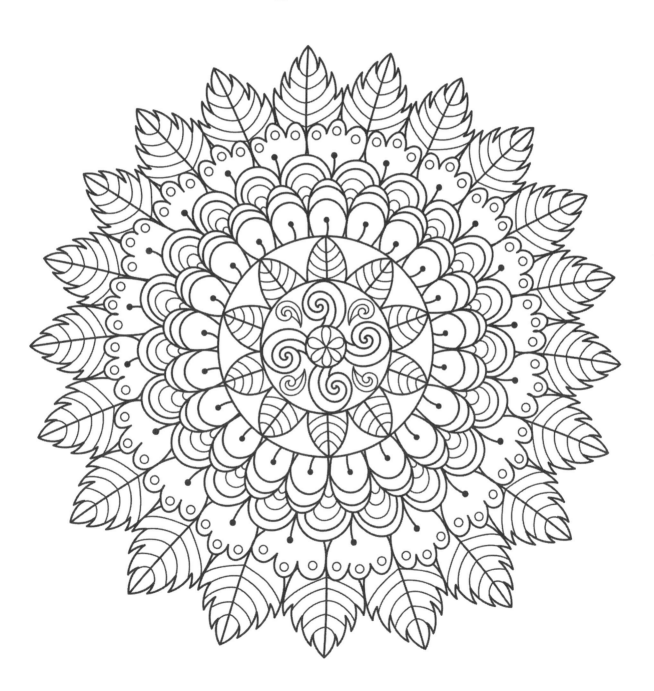

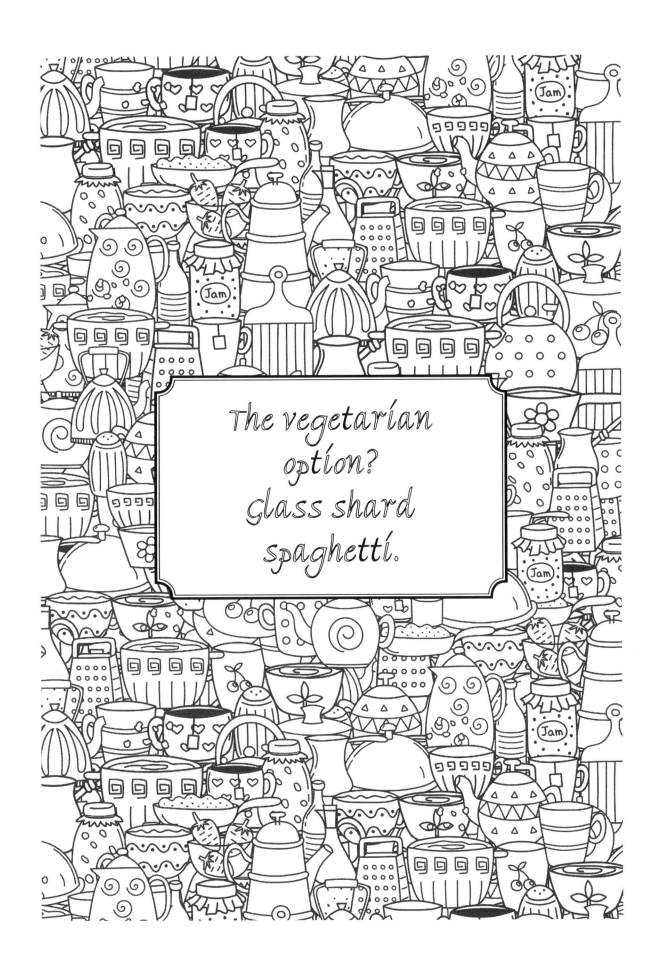

The vegetarian
option?
Glass shard
spaghetti.

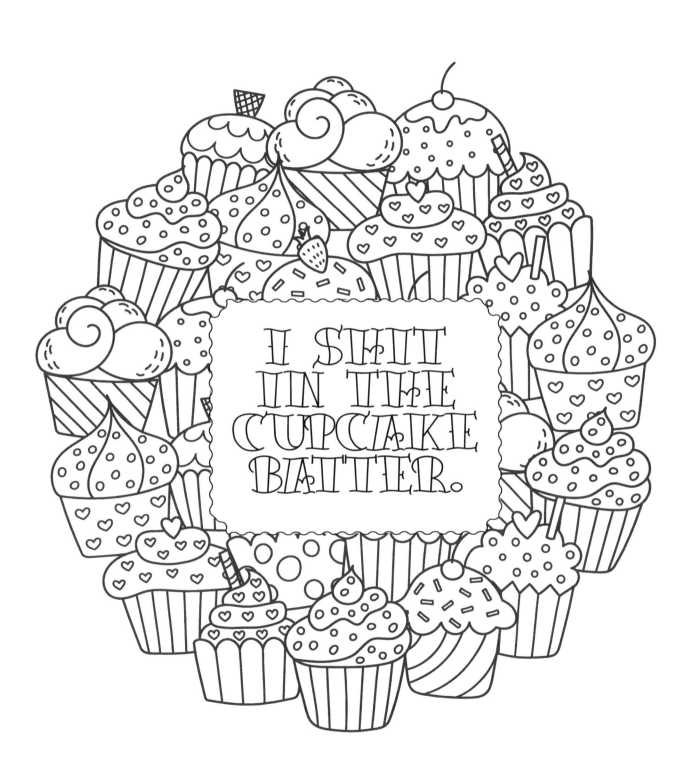

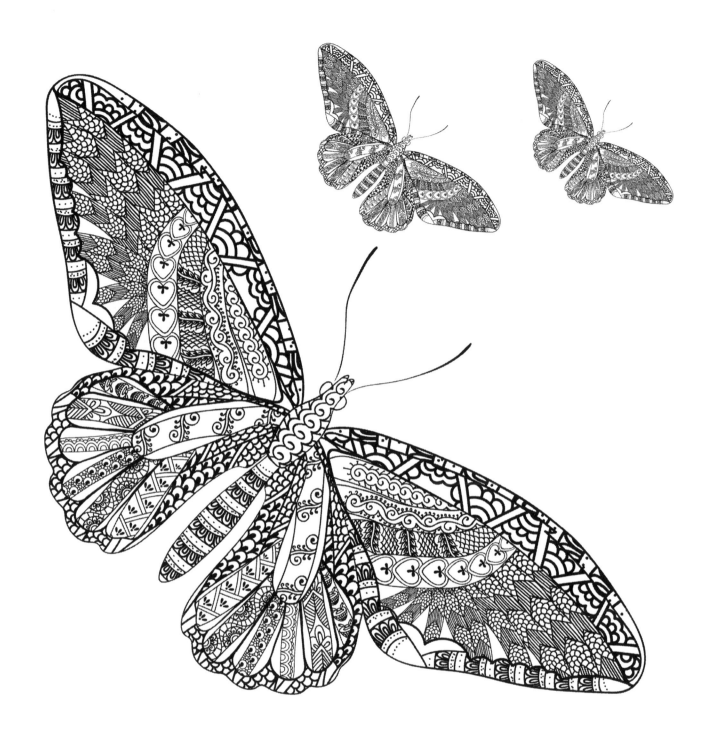

There it goes...
the last fuck I give.

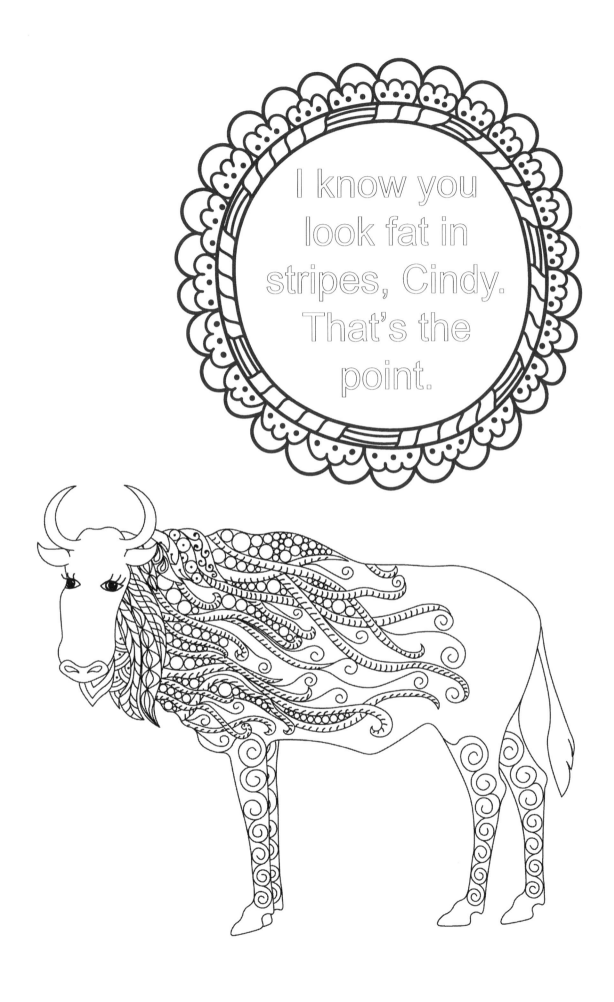

I know you look fat in stripes, Cindy. That's the point.

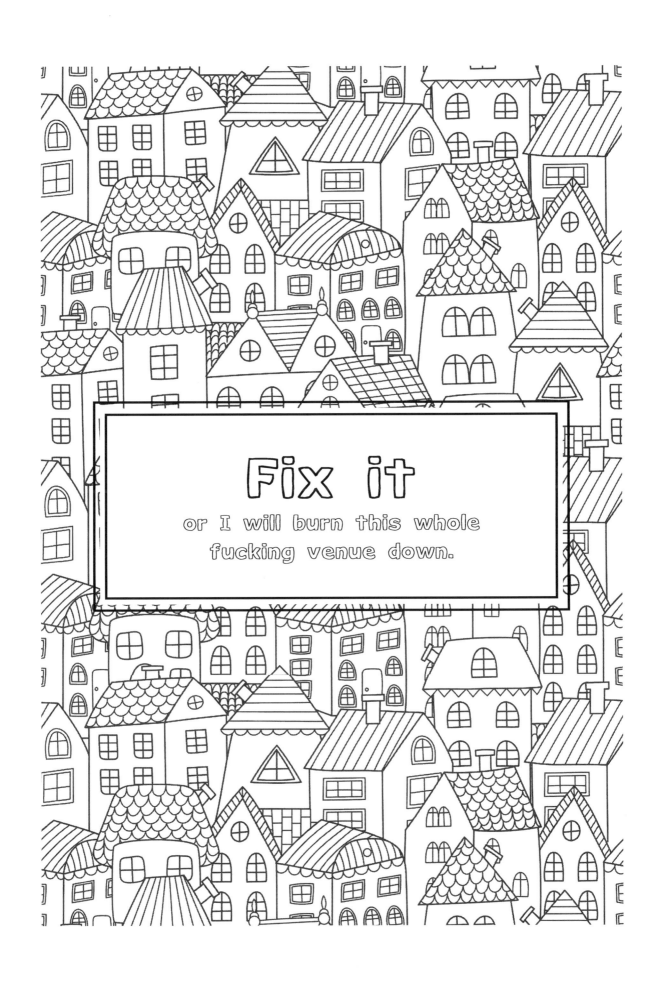

Fix it

or I will burn this whole
fucking venue down.

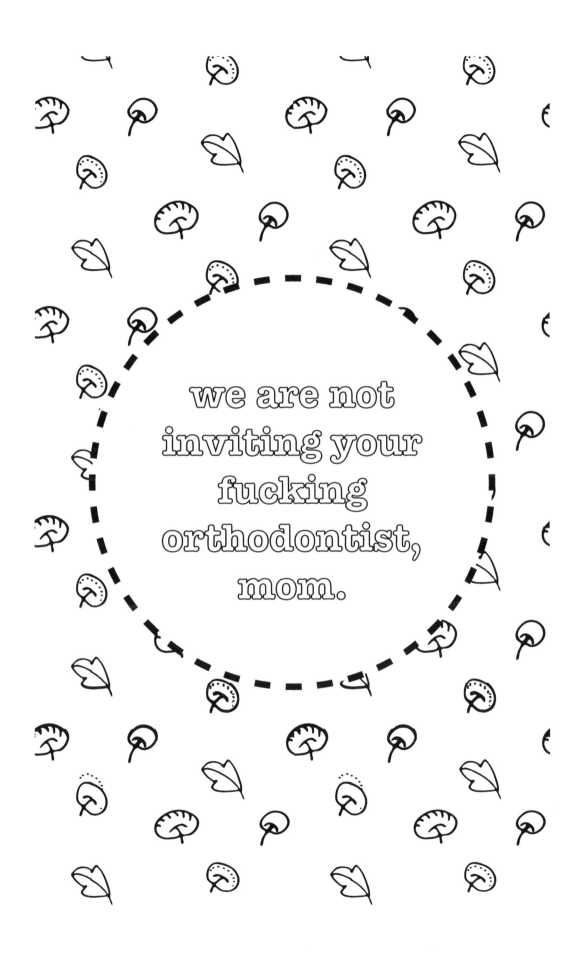

we are not
inviting your
fucking
orthodontist,
mom.

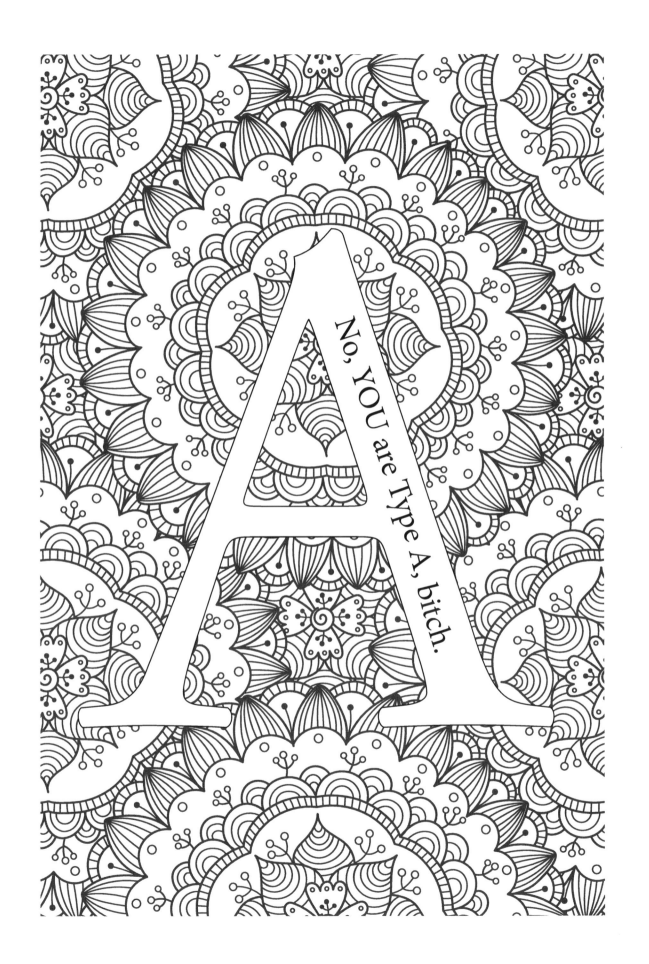

No, YOU are Type A, bitch.

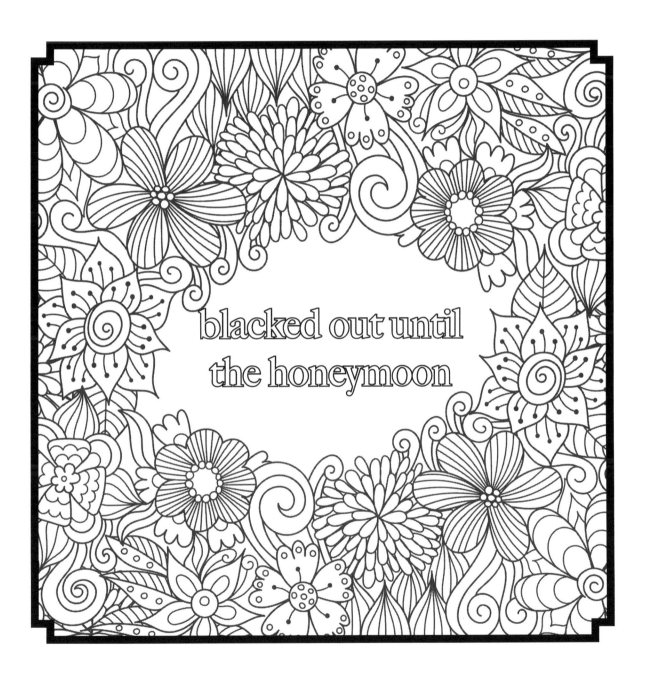

blacked out until
the honeymoon

Did you enjoy this coloring book?

If so, would you consider paying it forward by leaving a review on Amazon?

A review is the best way to help me spread the word about this book, and hopefully it will help the next bride color her way back to sanity, too!

To leave a review:

Google search "eat drink and fuck that shit coloring book" and click the first Amazon link.
Or, copy this URL into your browser: TK.

This should take you to the Amazon book page, where you can leave a review.

Thank you so much, and congratulations!

Gift a book = spread hope!

Coloring has been shown to alleviate stress and reduce anxiety, but not everybody can color their way back to feeling better. That's why we've committed to donating 10% of the proceeds of this book to the Brain and Behavior Research Foundation, which helps fund scientific research for mental health. So just by buying this book, you've helped fund research to help those struggling with mental illness—thank you so much for that.

To spread the love even more, you can also gift a copy of this book to a friend. They'll love you for it, and you'll be making a difference in someone's life!

To gift a book:

Google search "eat drink and fuck that shit coloring book" and click the first Amazon link.

Or, copy this URL into your browser: TK.

This should take you to the book page, where on the right, you'll see a button that says "Give as a Gift."

Happy gifting!

18985148R00031

Made in the USA
San Bernardino, CA
23 December 2018